MAR 0 6 2017

United States Regions

Southern Region

L.L. Owens

Rourke
Educational Media

rourkeeducationalmedia.com

Scan for Related Titles
and Teacher Resources

Before Reading:

Building Academic Vocabulary and Background Knowledge

Before reading a book, it is important to tap into what your child or students already know about the topic. This will help them develop their vocabulary, increase their reading comprehension, and make connections across the curriculum.

1. Look at the cover of the book. What will this book be about?
2. What do you already know about the topic?
3. Let's study the Table of Contents. What will you learn about in the book's chapters?
4. What would you like to learn about this topic? Do you think you might learn about it from this book? Why or why not?
5. Use a reading journal to write about your knowledge of this topic. Record what you already know about the topic and what you hope to learn about the topic.
6. Read the book.
7. In your reading journal, record what you learned about the topic and your response to the book.
8. After reading the book complete the activities below.

Content Area Vocabulary
Read the list. What do these words mean?

agriculture

arts

climate

culture

equality

geography

industry

prehistoric

region

settlers

tourism

After Reading:

Comprehension and Extension Activity

After reading the book, work on the following questions with your child or students in order to check their level of reading comprehension and content mastery.

1. Which state in the Southern region is the oldest? (Summarize)
2. Why do you think the post-war time is called Reconstruction? (Infer)
3. What feature of the South appeals to you? Why? (Text to self connection)
4. Explain antebellum architecture. (Summarize)
5. How did the state of Georgia get its name? (Summarize)

Extension Activity

During the Civil War, people in some families fought on different sides. It was not uncommon to see father against son or brother against brother on a battlefield. This difference in beliefs often tore families apart. Imagine you are a teenage boy living in the South. The Civil War has started and you disagree with your father's beliefs, so you decide to run away and join the Union army. Write a letter to your family explaining your decision. What would you say? Would you ever come back home? Was this difficult for you to write? Share your letter and experience writing it with your classmates.

Table of Contents

Where Is the South?

Let's explore the American South. That's the name of a United States area, or **region**. If you like **geography**, you may know that the region is located in the southern part of the country.

Geography is the study of Earth's physical features. Those include land, air, water, and life forms. Geography is one of our oldest sciences.

The special features of a region's geography help tell its story. They tie in to how people live and work in the region now. They also offer clues about why people came to live there and where they came from.

The South is an important region in the United States. Each region has similar traits found across the area. States in the South include Arkansas, Louisiana, Mississippi, Alabama, Georgia, Kentucky, Tennessee, and Missouri.

Louisiana Swamp

Triple Falls, Arkansas

Rickwood Caverns, Alabama

Kentucky Horse Farm

Georgia Live Oak Trees

7

Historical Beginnings

Georgia is the oldest state in the South. It was one of the original thirteen colonies. It became the fourth state in the Union in 1788. That happened more than two centuries ago! The youngest state in the South is Arkansas. It joined the Union in 1836.

The Mound Builders are the earliest known peoples to live in the long-ago South. They are the ancient ancestors of several Native Indian tribes.

Rock Eagle Effigy Mound in Putnam County, Georgia.

British, French, and Spanish **settlers** were some of the first people to come to the South. They started arriving in the eighteenth century. But they weren't the first to call the region home. Native peoples had lived there since **prehistoric** times.

9

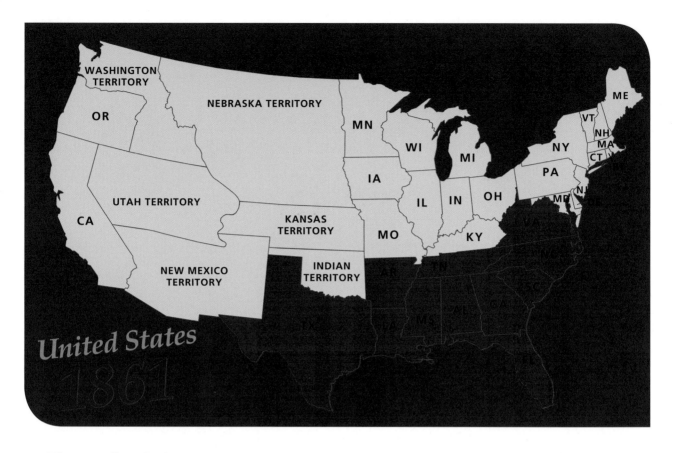

The 11 Confederate states were: Alabama, Arkansas, Florida, Georgia, Louisiana, Mississippi, North Carolina, Tennessee, Texas, South Carolina, and Virginia.

The Civil War era was a hard time in U.S. history. It began in 1860 and 1861 as eleven states seceded from, or left, the United States. Most were in the South. These states disagreed with President Abraham Lincoln's ideas. So they formed their own separate country. They called their new nation the Confederate States of America.

Lincoln didn't want the United States to split in two. But the Confederates believed in their right to create their own government. That's when they declared war.

Abraham Lincoln (1809–1865)

Battle of Williamsburg, May 5, 1862

The Civil War is known by several names. The War Between the States is common. The saddest name is the War Between Brothers. Many family members fought on opposite sides. Other names for the war are:
· War Between the North and the South
· War of the Rebellion
· War of Northern Aggression

The American Civil War raged for four long years. In 1865, the South surrendered to the North. The Confederate states would remain in the United States.

The South suffered the most damage in the war. Many bloody battles had been fought there. It would take years to rebuild all the homes, businesses, and farms that had been destroyed. Even the state governments needed rebuilding. This post-war time is called the Reconstruction.

The Bloodiest War in American History
More than 600,000 soldiers died during the Civil War. The United States has been involved in many other wars, but none have resulted in so many American deaths.

Birmingham, Alabama was founded after the Civil War in 1871. Mining, railroads, and the steel industry helped turn it into the great city it is today.

Fortunately, the South recovered from the Civil War's damage. It took time, but its citizens pulled together and created the beautiful, thriving region that exists today.

Getting Down to Business

Industry refers to a place's business activity. One of the most important Southern industries is **agriculture**. That's the business of farming crops and growing livestock.

Main crops in the region include rice, soybeans, cotton, and sugarcane. Other crops are tobacco, corn, hay, wheat, sweet potatoes, pecans, and peanuts.

Georgia is so famous for growing peaches that its nickname is the Peach State. Recently, though, it has been producing more blueberry crops than peach crops! Southern livestock farmers raise a variety of animals. They include chickens, turkeys, cattle, hogs, horses, and mules.

Cotton is one of the Southern region's most successful crops.

Manufacturing is the business of making products in factories. It's another important Southern industry. Chemicals, automobiles, airplanes, processed foods, furniture, and paper products are just some of the items made in the South.

Another big Southern industry is **tourism**. The comfortable **climate** makes visiting easier and more enjoyable.

Each year, more than 600,000 people visit Graceland in Memphis, Tennessee. It's Elvis Presley's former home. Now it serves as the King of Rock and Roll's official museum.

The Tuskegee Airmen National Historic Site in Alabama honors a group of African-American World War II pilots. They fought for the world's freedom and their own **equality**.

Another Southern draw is the annual Kentucky Derby horse race in Louisville, Kentucky.

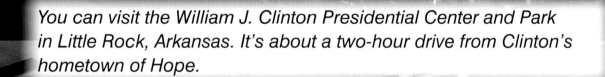

You can visit the William J. Clinton Presidential Center and Park in Little Rock, Arkansas. It's about a two-hour drive from Clinton's hometown of Hope.

Cultural Bits and Pieces

A region's history is seen in its modern **culture**. Some cultural elements have grown out of the South's rich past.

Language

Languages spoken in the South came from its natives and settlers. Native American tribal languages, such as Quapaw and Choctaw were once widely spoken.

Louisiana is a unique melting pot of spoken language. Some people speak Louisiana Creole. That has its roots in French, African, and native languages.

Place names can reflect the cultural and geographical heritage of its inhabitants. British settlers named Georgia after King George II of England. French settlers chose the name Arkansas. It came from the Sioux word acansa, which means "downstream place."

The Mardi Gras celebration in Louisiana combines the culture of the people who live there.

Architecture

One architectural style found in the South is called antebellum, which means prewar. Most antebellum homes were built before the Civil War. The grand style of mansion was often found on large plantations.

The Arts

Regional **arts** can mean just about anything people create. Think of books, paintings, music, dance, sculpture, and more.

Music is a defining art form in the South. It played a big part in the region's cultural history and is still a huge force today. Many American musical styles started in the region. They include blues, country, rock and roll, gospel, and jazz.

The Ryman Auditorium in Nashville, Tennessee is the original building that housed the Grand Ole Opry. The Opry has presented the biggest stars in country music since 1925.

Cheesy Baked Catfish

Catfish is a traditional Southern food. This easy, cheesy recipe is sure to please the whole family! Be sure to ask an adult to help you prepare it.

Cheesy Baked Catfish

Ingredients:

1 egg, beaten

$\frac{1}{2}$ cup milk

1 cup grated Parmesan cheese

$\frac{1}{2}$ cup flour

1 teaspoon paprika

$\frac{1}{2}$ teaspoon black pepper

$\frac{1}{4}$ teaspoon seasoning salt

$\frac{1}{4}$ teaspoon garlic powder

6 boneless, skinless catfish

$\frac{1}{4}$ cup melted butter

Directions:

1. Preheat the oven to 350 degrees. Then coat a 9 x 13-inch baking dish with cooking spray.

2. In a medium bowl, stir together the egg and milk.

3. Combine the next six dry ingredients in a separate bowl.

4. Dip one catfish into the egg mixture to coat. Then gently dip it into the dry mixture. Place it on the baking dish. Repeat this process for all catfish pieces.

5. Sprinkle extra paprika and black pepper over the fish.

6. Bake the catfish for 40 minutes.

State Facts Sheet

Arkansas

Motto: The People Rule.

Nickname: The Natural State

Capital: Little Rock

Known for: America's Only Diamond Mine, Hot Springs National Park, Former President Bill Clinton

Fun Fact: Sam Walton opened his first Walmart stores in Bentonville.

Louisiana

Motto: Union, Justice, and Confidence.

Nickname: The Pelican State

Capital: Baton Rouge

Known for: Jazz Music, Mardi Gras, Cajun Food

Fun Fact: Louisiana is the only state that does not have counties; its land is divided into parishes.

Mississippi

Motto: By Valor and Arms.

Nickname: The Magnolia State

Capital: Jackson

Known for: Mississippi River Boats, Antebellum Mansions

Fun Fact: In 1884, a Vicksburg shoe parlor was the first ever to sell shoes in pairs.

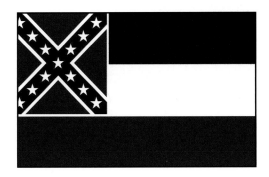

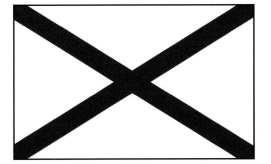

Alabama

Motto: We Dare Maintain our Rights.

Nickname: The Heart of Dixie

Capital: Montgomery

Known for: Beaches, Cotton

Fun Fact: For a short time, Montgomery was the capital of the Confederate States of America.

Georgia

Motto: Wisdom, Justice, and Moderation.
Nickname: The Peach State
Capital: Atlanta
Known for: Centennial Olympic Park,
Peaches
Fun Fact: Coca-Cola was invented in
1886 by an Atlanta pharmacist.

Kentucky

Motto: United We Stand, Divided
We Fall.
Nickname: The Bluegrass State
Capital: Frankfort
Known for: Kentucky Derby,
Mammoth Cave National Park
Fun Fact: Kentucky bluegrass is
not really blue, it's green. But
its buds are a bluish-purple in
the spring.

Did you know that Arkansas,
Mississippi, and Tennessee all
have the same state bird? The
mockingbird enjoys the Southern
climate and lives in the region
year round.

Tennessee

Motto: Agriculture and Commerce.

Nickname: The Volunteer State

Capital: Nashville

Known for: Great Smoky Mountains, Grand Ole Opry, Graceland

Fun Fact: A replica of Davy Crockett's log cabin stands on the banks of Limestone Creek.

Missouri

Motto: The Welfare of the People Shall Be the Supreme Law.

Nickname: The Show-Me State

Capital: Jefferson City

Known for: First Ice-Cream Cone Invented at World's Fair in 1904

Fun Fact: Kansas City is rumored to have more fountains than any city except Rome.

Branson, Missouri, is known for the many concerts, magic acts, plays, and other shows it offers each year. This makes Branson a perfect fit within The Show-Me State!

Glossary

agriculture (AG-ri-kuhl-chur): the raising of crops and animals

arts (ahrts): making and sharing works of art

climate (KLYE-mit): the everyday weather of a place

culture (KUHL-chur): the way of life for a group of people

equality (i-KWAH-li-tee): having the same rights as others

geography (jee-AH-gruh-fee): the physical features of a place

industry (IN-duh-stree): businesses found in a community

prehistoric (pree-hi-STOR-ik): before recorded history

region (REE-juhn): a specific geographic area

settlers (SET-lurz): people who create homes in a new place

tourism (TOOR-izm): visiting a place for pleasure

Index

Show What You Know

1. Which states in the South also cross into other regions?
2. Who was president during the Civil War?
3. How long did the Civil War last?
4. Why is Georgia called the Peach State?
5. Where did the name Arkansas come from?

Websites to Visit

www.ducksters.com/history/civilwartimeline.php

www.elvis.com/about-the-king/for_kids.aspx

www.eduplace.com/kids/socsci/books/applications/imaps/maps/
g4n_u3/

Author

Originally from the Midwest, L.L. Owens now lives in the Pacific Northwest. She has written more than 80 books for children and loves working with both nonfiction and fiction. Learn more about her at www.llowens.com.

Meet The Author!
www.meetREMauthors.com

PHOTO CREDITS: Cover: © dina2001, matthewleesdixon, mstroz, rarena, JacobH; Page 1: © Sean Pavone; Page 3: © Steve Bower; Page 5–6: © Visions of America LLC; Page 7: © Steve Brigman, Jason Ross, Alexey Stiop, Darryl Brooks; Page 8–9: © Library of Congress; Page 11: © The Print Collector; Page 12–13: © Hulton Archive; Page 14: © Library of Congress; Page 15: © Sean Pavone; Page 16: © Shank_ali; Page 17: © Kletr; Page 18: © Cheryl Ann Quigley; Page 19: © Henry Sadura, Nagel Photography; Page 21: © DHuss; Page 22: © adpower99; Page 23: © Paul Giamou, Alex Master; Page 24: © HKPNC; Page 25: © Natalia K

Edited by: Jill Sherman

Cover design by: Jen Thomas
Interior design by: Rhea Magaro

Library of Congress PCN Data

Southern Region / L.L. Owens
(United States Regions)
ISBN 978-1-62717-675-0 (hard cover)
ISBN 978-1-62717-797-9 (soft cover)
ISBN 978-1-62717-914-0 (e-Book)
Library of Congress Control Number: 2014934383

Also Available as:

Printed in the United States of America, North Mankato, Minnesota